MY STORY

ISABELLA ISITORO

MY STORY

To Anne D. Sears

Isabella Isitoro

"Thank you"

Copyright © 2017 by Isabella Isitoro.

Library of Congress Control Number: 2017900875
ISBN: Hardcover 978-1-5245-7713-1
Softcover 978-1-5245-7712-4
eBook 978-1-5245-7711-7

All rights reserved. No part of this book may be reproduced or transmitted in any form or by any means, electronic or mechanical, including photocopying, recording, or by any information storage and retrieval system, without permission in writing from the copyright owner.

Any people depicted in stock imagery provided by Thinkstock are models, and such images are being used for illustrative purposes only.
Certain stock imagery © Thinkstock.

Print information available on the last page.

Rev. date: 02/14/2017

To order additional copies of this book, contact:
Xlibris
1-888-795-4274
www.Xlibris.com
Orders@Xlibris.com
753407

PRELUDE

This book is a true story about some of my experiences while living through World War II and beyond.

To my late mother Hermine who endured so very much throughout the war and to my stepfather Wladimir who helped to provide and make a better life possible.

Also to my friend Betty (Elizabeth Lutz), who has been instrumental and encouraged me continuously for a long time to write about my life experiences since I once shared them with her.

The beginning of my story is what my mother shared with me, because it took place before my arrival.

My mother was born in Germany and grew up with her parents living near the Austrian border because my grandfather was a border control officer and my grandmother was a homemaker.

After my grandfather passed away, my grandmother decided to move to central Germany to a suburb in the outskirts of Munich called Pasing to be closer to her family.

In Pasing, a streetcar traveled back and forth to downtown Munich where my grandmother loved to shop.

My father was born and grew up in Vienna, Austria. He was a private pilot and was employed by a large distribution corporation.

My mother was employed as a private secretary for a large manufacturing corporation that had a business contract with my father's distribution company, and this is where they met.

Unfortunately, I do not remember much about many of my relatives, because some passed away before I came along and many succumbed during the war.

I vividly remember my grandmother, who was my mother's mother, because during the war I had to live with her when my mother was assigned government duties.

After my mother and father were married, my mother stopped working and became a homemaker.

One sunny weekend, they decided to take a walk to a park that was located not far from home, and as they walked past the police station they noticed a cute fox terrier for sale in the window. They decided to go inside to inquire about him and ended up taking him home.

They named him Schnucki, who turned out to be well-behaved, obedient as well as housebroken.

However, after a while my mother noticed that every now and then Schnucki would sneak away for a bit of time but always returned back home again. This made her curious and she decided to follow him one day to see where he went. To her surprise, he walked to the square and hopped on the streetcar to Munich.

When the next streetcar arrived she questioned the conductor if he knew anything about a fox terrier hopping on the streetcar to Munich? Surprisingly, the conductor was aware of this and informed her that the dog formerly belonged to a madam at the Munich

Bordello, but the police took him away from her and since then he has been visiting her occasionally.

Later that day when my father came home, she told him what she found out, and after some discussion, they decided to keep him anyway because he was such nice pet.

Then . . . the unthinkable happened, I came along. When my parents brought me home, Schnucki was all excited and preoccupied with keeping watch over me.

Schnucki became very protective to the point where he would even sleep under the crib, and if I cried he would bark until I was attended to. Even his travels to Munich became much less frequent and would only sneak off once in a while for a short period of time. He was constantly near me like a guardian.

When the time came for me to start kindergarten, my mother would walk me to school, and of course Schnucki would also accompany us. However, after my mother dropped me off, he refused to go home with her and parked himself under a tree nearby. My mother figured that since he knew how to travel to

Munich he would also find his way home and left him there.

After my mother was out of sight, he would then approach the school entrance and search for me. Back then, all doors had L-shaped door handles and this made it very easy for him to open doors. All he had to do was hit the L and the door would open.

Once he found where I was, he would enter the classroom and park himself under my chair. The teacher who was a nun tried to coax him out of the classroom, but he started to growl, snarl, and bark at her. Since she did not want to disrupt or scare the whole class, she left him there as long as he did not interfere in any way.

However, later that day the nun called my mother and requested that she come to school to discuss a problem with her.

After my mother and the nun had a lengthy discussion at school, it was decided that Schnucki would be allowed to attend kindergarten with me, but only if he was nondisruptive in any way.

Since this was a time when many rumors were being discussed about a pending war, people as well as businesses were either preparing their basements or building underground bunkers. This no doubt had a lot to do with the schools decision to allow Schnucki to come to kindergarten with me.

It was absolutely an atmosphere of nervousness, uncertainty, and insecurity.

I only wish I had some pictures of Schnucki and me in the classroom, but unfortunately they were lost when my grandmother's home was bombed later on in the war.

Approximately five or six months later the bombing attacks began here and there on a daily basis.

Unfortunately, several weeks later, my grandmother's home was demolished during one of the bombing attacks. Luckily, no one was home when it happened.

Schnucki and I were at school, my mother and grandmother were out shopping, and my father was at work.

Needless to say, it was very upsetting to come home and find a big pile of rubble on the ground, with nowhere to go.

Therefore, for the next week we had to stay at a shelter until my parents were able to find new living quarters.

Fortunately, they found one apartment for us located in the suburb of Pasing and another one for my grandmother that was not far from the Pasing Square close to stores and transportation.

Our apartment was a two-bedroom apartment on the second floor of a private home.

My grandmother's was a one-bedroom unit on the second floor of a former Biergarden Resort Hotel.

The resort hotel still maintained the first floor, operating the restaurant, the Biergarden, as well as all the other amenities, which included the swimming pool with lounge chairs, change cabins with showers, and bowling on the green, which is a game similar to boccie but on grass.

Also a medium-sized river ran alongside the left border of the property called the Wurm (worm), where one could also go swimming. The back as well as the right side of the property was fenced.

The property behind the fence belonged to a large hospital that grew various vegetables along with several fruit trees. All of the produce was used to feed their hospital patients.

Near the back fence the resort built an underground shelter for all of the tenants and guests.

Basically it was shaped like a large square wooden room with wooden benches all round, approximately fifteen feet long by seven feet wide and seven feet high.

On the right end of the shelter was a small compartment at the bottom that held an emergency first aid kit, a lantern, a radio, plus an electric outlet and a few blankets.

Above the compartment was a mock wooden hollow square window to serve as an escape hatch in case of an emergency.

On the left side end of the room was a door leading to a vestibule which had a mini bathroom along with a staircase for the entry and exit into the shelter.

On top of the shelter was a wooden roof with about two or three feet of soil and grass. The vestibule area had the same roof but that section of the roof was on a sliding track to allow entry and exit.

Life seemed as routinely as possible, along with running to shelters every time the alarms sounded which always was quite interrupting and worrisome.

When the time came for me to attend first grade, which luckily was in the same building as the kindergarten class, my mother set up an appointment with the superintendent to discuss the Schnucki problem.
After a lengthy discussion it was decided that Schnucki was allowed to accompany me to first grade.
I believe that this decision was mainly due to the fact that everyone was struggling with the war and that Schnucki was exceptionally well-behaved.

Me in first grade

My father, mother, and Schucki

A short time later, we received two certified letters, one addressed to my mother, the other to my father, informing my mother that she will be assigned government duties and that my father was going to be drafted within the next few weeks.

My mother tried to appeal her assignment, but she was told that since her mother was still living who could take care of me during the day, she will be assigned to assist with certain government duties, especially while most men are being drafted.

After both my parents received their assignments, I began to stay with my grandmother.

I loved staying with Grandmom because she spoiled me more than my mother.

Since my mother worked long hours, my grandmother suggested that I should stay at her place full-time and that my mother should have dinner with us every day to spend time with us before going home to her apartment.

My mother agreed to the proposal and thanked my grandmother for the offer.

One evening while having dinner, my mother told us that she was assigned assembly work at a special manufacturing company that manufactured high-speed zoom lens spy cameras for airplanes.

She further informed us that she was required to sign secrecy documentation not to discuss her duties with anyone; otherwise this could create severe consequences for her. Besides that, she was also searched when she arrived for work as well as when she left for the day.

Naturally, we never talked about her work assignments with anyone. If anyone did ask, we would only say that she was doing routine assembly work.

Late one afternoon the hotel building manager knocked on our door and handed us a framed picture of Hitler and instructed us that we needed to hang it near our entrance door so that when someone enters our unit it could be seen.

He also informed us that he is required to give a picture to every tenant in the building, plus he must make periodic checks to make certain everyone complies.

He then turned to me and said that if I am well-behaved, he will sneak me some goodies from the restaurant plus allow me to use the leisure facilities.

This certainly was a very good reason for me to be on my best behavior.

As time went on, more restrictions and control was imposed little by little. People became more distant of one another because one never knew which side of the fence they supported, in order to avoid any hassles or get reported to the Gestapo.
We never attended any parades or rallies and was kept from as much of the political gatherings as possible.

In the spring of 1942 my mother received a telegram notifying her that my father was shot down near a town called Briansk located by the Russian Border and that the plane blew up.
This of course was terrible news, especially since we had not seen him since he was drafted.
After my mother held a memorial service for my father, she decided to give up their apartment and move in with us.

A little while later, food and other staples became more scarce, and the government ruled that food ration cards were going to be issued. I remember that there were three types: heavy duty, medium, and regular, and they would be assigned according to the type of work one performed. Naturally, we were only assigned the regular ones.

This meant that our ration cards did not include butter, sugar, and the like, with meat only once a month.

Instead of butter, we were entitled to lard, instead of sugar, saccharin, along with several other poorer substitutes.
We were able to get potatoes, carrots, spinach, cabbage, flour, farina along with seasonal fruits like apples, pears and grapes though.

Seasonally, my grandmother and I would go wild berry picking, and she then would make some jams which was a real treat.
Having a slice of bread with some lard and jam seemed like a luxury so were baked potatoes with lard.

Once a month my grandmother and I would have to go downtown to pick up our assigned ration cards and the lines were always quite long.

On one occasion while standing in a long line to pick up our monthly assigned ration cards, I noticed a large box under the dispensing person's desk. While my grandmother presented our identity verification cards, I reached down and took a few and tucked them into my coat pocket.

As we walked out of the building to go home, I became very nervous and scared, silently praying that no one saw me doing that.

After we arrived at home, I was afraid to tell my grandmother as to what I had done, but when my mother came home from work I confessed.

At first she scolded me and made me promise to never do anything like that again because if caught or reported, we could all be severely punished.

A while later when my mother looked at the ration cards, she noticed that they were the medium type. She immediately grabbed her purse and went to go to Munich to shop. However, she went to a totally different area of Munich, where she had never shopped before, to make absolutely sure no one would recognize her. Also, she only purchased nonperishable items and nothing that needed to be cooked, because cooking odors could emanate from the apartment and some faithful Nazi person may report us, causing an investigation by the Gestapo. She also made several trips in order not to make anyone suspicious by carrying too many packages. That was sadly how it was during that time.

After my mother finished shopping, she became quite nervous for some time hoping that she would not get caught.

Thank God, neither one of us was ever reported.

Actually, we had quite a few nice items which we hid in the cedar closet and could have shared some with others. However, times were such as mentioned earlier, one could not take the chance or risk of getting reported and jailed.

By this time, the sirens were steadily increasing more often and this became quite disruptive.

Classes at school began to place more emphasis on reading, writing, math, religion, and patriotic lectures. All other subjects were either cut or only taught if or when time allowed.

Periodically we received survival instructions at school in case we were somewhere and unable to get to a shelter, like lying flat on the ground and covering your head with your arms, or if near soft ground, digging a hole and placing your face inside the hole and covering your head with your arms.
This helps to protect you from flying objects or inhaling harmful fumes.

We were also instructed to never pick up any toys, gift-wrapped items, or aluminum-type items because they were booby traps that detonate when picked up or even touched; all are capable to maim or kill a person.

One early morning on a weekend, the sirens were really sounding very loud; everyone in the building was rushing to get to the shelter in the back of the Biergarden ground. One of the tenants, an elderly man, would always stay in the vestibule area to allow him to smoke his pipe, because the ceiling in that area had a sliding track and this allowed him to slide it a bit open near the staircase of the bunker.

Somehow, a sharp pilot must have noticed something and began bombing the left side of the bunker area. This blew out the escape window and the door, and the ceiling caved in on us.

Everyone did his or her best to remove the dirt, grass, boards, truss, etc., so that we could at least breathe. We remained still for a while to make sure that the plane did not return before we continued to remove all the rest of the debris around us.
Even Schnucki managed to get himself out.
Unfortunately, the pipe smoker did not survive.

Immediately, the Biergarden began to make arrangements to have the bunker rebuilt.

Then several weeks later, someone came to our door to tell us that Schnucki was accidentally run over by a car and killed while crossing the street.

Apparently Schnucki was coming back from Munich and in a hurry to get home.

My grandmother immediately walked to the square and picked up his body before a dumpster would collect him.

After my mother came home from work, we buried him in the very back of the property and we held a ceremony for him.

I was terribly heartbroken and cried for quite some time. After all, I had spent my whole life with him. He was always by my side protecting me no matter what, and now he was gone.

Then some weeks later my mother received a notice to appear in court. However, the notice did not list any reason.

The day my mother went to court in Munich to find out what this was all about, she never returned home. Therefore, my grandmother kept me home from school and took me with her to Munich to find out what happened to my mother.

After a lengthy wait, we were finally able to see the magistrate who informed us that my mother was serving six months in jail because she had committed a crime. It seemed that two coworkers observed my mother embracing a prisoner of war behind a door at work and reported her to the Gestapo.

When my mother finished her sentence and returned home, she was no longer allowed back to work at the same place. Instead she was reassigned to a military dry cleaning plant with a lower salary.

Everything for a while seemed to be going as routinely as possible, while still running in and out of bomb shelters. Until one day my mother received a call at work notifying her that my grandmother had fallen down a flight of stairs and was taken to the hospital.

When my mother arrived at the hospital she was informed that my grandmother had a broken spine, and back then there was nothing they could do for her, especially since she was in her midnineties. She passed away shortly thereafter.

My Grandmother

During the war no personal funeral viewings were held as we know them. Instead the government built several one-floor buildings in various areas. Each building generally had ten small individual showcase rooms.

The buildings were named Leichenhaus (deathhouse).

There in each room a declared dead person was displayed in an open casket, with a name plate and dates at the bottom. Any maimed person would not be displayed and would have a closed casket church service and burial.

When my grandmother passed away, my mother took me with her to pay our last respects. We also would go, when one of our relatives died.

It was customary that the exhibit would display a person who died under normal conditions for two days; however, a person who died during a bombing would be on display for four to five days. This was mainly due to the fact that even though they were declared dead at the time, every so often a person on display in the showcase would all of a sudden wake up. This was called Scheintot (artificially dead), an abnormal cataleptic trance.

Sometimes it seemed like tragedies never end and losing my grandmother was another.

My mother took care of all the burial arrangements and buried my grandmother with my grandfather in the cemetery plot which they had originally purchased.

Now that grandmother was gone, the government had to release my mother from her work assignment to take care of me, and this was a good thing.

With all that had happened to us, my mother was very worn out. Therefore, she decided that we get away for a little while and spend some time on a farm south of us.

Somehow, I cannot remember the name of the farm area or the name of the town.

The first week on the farm was very enjoyable, with nice people and good food, plus peaceful surroundings.

One morning on a really nice sunny day, my mother decided that we should walk to the town nearby and see what it looked like. The town only had two stores, a country store and a hardware store, along with a nice park with a pond and a couple of benches where we went to sit and watch nature for a while.

As we prepared to return to the farm, we decided to take a shortcut and walked between the wheat and cornfield.

However, halfway back to the farm, one of the heels of my mother's shoes broke off, and as she looked around she could hear machinery running in a building not far from us and decided that we should walk there and let them nail the heel back on.

As we approached the building, we were arrested, fingerprinted, interrogated, and questioned as to what we were doing there. After my mother explained to them why we were there, they made her sign a statement of secrecy and instructed her to have a talk with me. Then they did nail her heel on to the shoe and allowed us to leave.

Later at the dinner table with the farmers, we briefly mentioned to them what had happened to us on the way back to the farm from town. They informed us that all the farmers surrounding the building had to sign secrecy statements because it was a government military research and manufacturing center for artillery, ammunition, as well as a missile assembly plant.

The next time we went to town, we definitely did not take any shortcut again, but this time on our way back, I could hear a plane in the distance, and for some reason I became very frightened and nervous, and I begged my mother to please run toward a large tree ahead of us. At first my mother tried to calm me down, but I kept insisting until she finally agreed and we ran toward the tree. Once there I felt safe, but now my mother became somewhat nervous.

My mother took off her overcoat that was a green tweed which by luck matched the grass surrounding us and instructed me to get down on the ground with her, then get under her coat behind her and together we will crawl over toward the large hedge several feet from the tree. Once there both of us will dig a hole and put our faces into the hole.
We had no sooner done that when we heard a loud bang, and as we looked out from under the hedge we saw that the tree was badly damaged.

After this episode my mother decided that what was happening to us in the country was just as upsetting as running to shelters in the city. Therefore we might as well go back home and take our chances there.

As we arrived back home in Pasing, there was a notice on our door from the post office that they were holding a package for us and to come and pick it up.

After my mother picked up the package and opened it, the package contained a Hitler Youth uniform along with instructions that I was going to be recruited into the Hitler Youth Training Program during my next year school enrollment and that she will be notified as to where and when to report with me.

This did not make my mother happy, but there was absolutely nothing whatsoever she could do about this.

By this time, the alarms were sounding more often than before, and we were spending more times in the shelter than before.

Because one could get killed just about anywhere anymore, no matter where you are, my mother decided one Saturday morning that we take a trip to Munich and shop a little.

As we returned to go back home and as we got off the streetcar at the Pasing Square, the sirens were blasting exceptionally loud and long, this meant that one needed to get to the nearest shelter possible.

Since a new shelter had been built near the square, we proceeded to go there and get in line. As we finally reached the entrance, the line was being cut off, because the shelter was filled to capacity. Luckily, we were part of the last few allowed entrance

As the door was closing behind us, I noticed that it was a very heavy and thick steel door, which reminded me of a bank vault door.

As a matter of fact, that shelter was a small version which resembled the Washington Monument in Washington, D.C. It had no windows, only the one heavy door entrance and exit. It had several floors with chairs to sit on; however it was not as tall.

When the bombing started, the shelter began to sway back and forth a lot and most people were falling off the chairs getting hurt or bruised including us.

Little did we know at the time that we would be locked up in the shelter for three and a half days and not be allowed to leave because the bombing was continuously ongoing around the clock.

During those three and a half days, most people began to sit and sleep on the floor, plus the water and food supply was getting scarce and limited and so were the facilities due to a bit of overcrowding.

However, after three and half days, an announcement was made that the war was over and that Germany had lost the war and that we were allowed to leave.

The very first thing we did was walk home to see if our building unit was still standing.
Once there we immediately took a bath. When my mother washed my hair, she noticed that I had picked up lice at the shelter.
She immediately arranged to have the apartment disinfected and then took me to a clinic where they washed my whole head with kerosene.

We were really glad that the war was over and felt very fortunate to have survived all the turmoil.

The memories walking back to our apartment was truly something I will never forget. There was not only just a lot of rubble to walk past but also a number of dead and maimed bodies here and there.

One good thing did happen and that was, that now with the war over, I would no longer be required to join the Hitler Youth Training Program which basically was nothing more than a brainwashing organization which we found out later on.

It was also after the war we heard the truth about what actually took place in Dachau regarding all the inhumane atrocities which made us ashamed and humiliated to admit that we were Germans.

I personally believe that many German people were not aware of what really took place there and those who did know were either threatened or afraid for their own lives.

A short time after the war, another phase or chapter began in an alarming way.
First, a battalion of Russians marched through our area, but they continued toward the north. Then a day later the American troops arrived and stayed and began to rape women. This created a terrible chaos

In order to prevent my mother from getting raped, we emptied part of the cedar closet in the bedroom where she hid inside during the day, since we never knew when one would come bursting into the building. I always opened our door whenever someone knocked or banged on it because if it was a soldier and I did not open the door, he would then just kick it open. Anytime, when one of them asked me "where is your mom," I would point to the main entrance downstairs. He would then go to next apartment.

Once in a while a soldier would walk through the apartment, but luckily none ever looked inside the closet.

Lucky for me, I was only a little past nine years old and was therefore left alone. I suppose if it were in today's times, it would be a different story.

After all the chaos stopped, the depression process began.

The German currency was depreciated three times over a period of a couple of months. After the dust settled, my mother lost almost all of her hard-earned money, and we started to have a really hard time living from day to day. However, we somehow managed the best we could for quite some time.

Then to our surprise one day, there was a knock on our door, and when my mother opened the door, there stood the war prisoner whom she embraced during the war. My mother was absolutely speechless and enormously surprised.

He informed my mother that after their embrace he was transferred to Austria doing hard labor work.

After my potential stepfather proposed to my mother and they were married, our standard of living improved somewhat.

A few months later my mother became pregnant, however, the baby was stillborn. This most likely attributed to the fact that she had lost a lot of weight and was also undernourished for some time.

Several months later my mother became pregnant again, and this time the baby was born with quite a few illnesses and spent her first two years in the hospital. At that time the hospital informed my parents that she was no longer responding to medication and that she may not survive. Therefore, they decided to bring her home and set up an around-the-clock schedule for all three of us.

To our surprise, little by little she started to perk up some and was also gaining a little weight. This was a good sign as well as a blessing.

She continued to improve and she is alive as I write this story.

Even though technically she is my stepsister, I consider her as my sister, and have always referred to her as my sister.

Several years later, my mother and stepfather were having a discussion where he proposed the possibility of migrating to the United States to start a new life to which my mother was very receptive. The following week my stepfather went to the American Consulate to apply to immigrate to the United States.

However, the American Consulate informed him that their immigration quota was closed for the year and he did not know when it would be activated again, nor could he accept any applications until further notice.

At the same time Australia was opening their immigration quota program. Therefore, my stepfather decided to apply there, because he was absolutely anxious to get out of Germany.

After he filed the application forms for all of us with the Australian Consulate, we were informed that we needed to have a complete physical and a clean criminal record and if approved the government would provide transportation with a two-year job commitment with the government by the breadwinner.

This seemed like a good offer and therefore he applied, and within two months we received the approval. We needed to be ready to leave in six weeks.

There was much to take care of in such a short time but somehow we managed it.

We left Germany and traveled by train to Senigallia, Italy.

When we arrived there we had to check in at a special immigration center, re-register, get vaccinated, and have another physical. After that we stayed overnight at a motel.

The next morning we left by bus and traveled to Naples, Italy and boarded a ship called the *Fairsea* an Orient Line cruise ship, and we traveled through the Suez

Canal, into the Indian Ocean toward the Fremantle Harbor in Western Australia.

We docked at the Fremantle Harbor in Western Australia on February 1950 which is approximately fifteen miles from Perth, the capital of Western Australia. A welcome committee was there to greet us and a bus was also waiting for us to take us to our destination, which was to a small town called Kelmscott about twenty miles south of Perth.

When we arrived in Kelmscott, we found a small community of Nissen unit buildings that the government provided for us. Each unit contained two bedrooms, one bathroom, a living room, and a kitchen with a wringer washer and refrigerator, plus each room had basic furniture. Also each unit was built on a small lot to allow us to hang our laundry and grow some vegetables or flowers.

(see picture on the next page)

An Australian friend and my sister and I

My stepfather, mother, sister, and I

After settling in for a couple of days, my stepfather was to begin working for the State Highway Department to satisfy the two-year agreement.

Next, I was assigned to a nearby high school, and the homemakers were requested to attend a weekly meeting to familiarize them with Australian customs and also learn the English language.

The high school class I was assigned to was staffed by Catholic nuns. All in all there were five immigrant girls, one was Hungarian, one was Estonian, two were Polish, and one was German (me), and our teacher requested us to sit in the very back of the class and asked us to listen.

Whenever the teacher gave her regular students assignments or tests, she would come to the back and tutor us.

She also informed us that we will be referred to as New Australians and not immigrants.

Also, each day we were requested to stay another hour after her regular students left to go home to allow for more personal tutoring.

After about four weeks later of part-time tutoring, the nun informed us that she received permission from some of the regular student parents as well as our own parents for each one of us to spend a few weekends as a guest at the home of an Australian family. This would help us adjust to our new lives and learn the language faster.

The student and the family that selected me had a very large farm, and that was exciting for me because I loved animals.
They had horses, cows, lambs, and chickens, along with various fruit trees and vegetable fields.

Helping with the animals was fun but so was fruit picking because I could nibble on some.
The farm also had a river that ran through their property, and during hot weather the student and I would go down to the river to swim and cool off. The only problem was that when we got out of the water, we always had to pull some leeches off of us that were attached on our legs. Also, I had to be careful and not stay in the sun too long because I always burned very easily.

It was absolutely amazing how fast I was learning English and adjusting to the Australian way of life. Therefore, after three months I was able to participate with the regular class, and so did the other girls.

Needless to say, sincere gratitude and thanks goes to the teacher who arranged the program and also to the Australian families who volunteered and so graciously devoted their time and effort to help us New Australians.

About a year later, I acquired a part-time job on weekends at a local country store where I prepared one, two, and three-pound bags of flour, sugar, rice, and cornmeal along with other staples. The pocket money sure came in handy.

After my stepfather's two-year commitment was fulfilled, we moved from the Nissen Unit in Kelmscott to a suburban area to a place called Victoria Park which was located just outside of Perth. Next he applied for a job at a wrought iron manufacturing company because he was a skilled wrought iron design maker, and they hired him immediately.

After I finished high school I was going to look for a job.

However, my stepfather insisted that I go to a business college and get a degree in business management.

He stressed that this was very important if I wanted to get ahead in life.

After I graduated from business college, I acquired a job as a bookkeeper with a furniture manufacturing company, whose headquarters were located in Sydney, Eastern Australia.

The office was only staffed with three employees in the office, the vice president, office manager, and me, the bookkeeper, along with twelve assemblers.

After working there for only a month, I noticed that the VP was hardly ever in the office, and we were receiving phone calls from women all over the globe who wanted to speak with him. Therefore I questioned the manager about this; she informed me that he was quite a ladies' man and that the home office never checks on him.

One day a vice president from the home office came to visit and asked to speak with our vice president. The manager informed him that we did not know, nor did we know where to contact him, because he always informed her that if he were in a conference he would not want to be disturbed, and that he would routinely contact and check in with us.

Well, this really disturbed the VP visitor and he immediately called his headquarters in Sydney.

The next morning when our VP arrived he was fired on the spot.

Therefore, the visiting VP temporarily filled the position until they hired someone else, and we always knew where to reach him if he went out.

The headquarter office in Sydney commended us for having done a great job under our previous circumstances and gave us both a salary increase.
However, at the same time they also reprimanded the office manager for not having reported this to them. They did not reprimand me, because I was a new employee.

Unfortunately, I did not work for the company for a very long time because my stepfather still had the United States on his mind and had already picked up applications to immigrate to the United States. The applications required that he have a job and housing available in order to get approval, plus we had to provide our own transportation.

Fortunately, during our years in Australia, my stepfather kept in touch with a friend of his who had immigrated to the United States years earlier, who was living in Trenton, New Jersey.

Therefore, he wrote to his friend to tell him that he was still thinking about moving to the United States but the American Consulate requested that he needed a commitment contract stating that he would be provided a job and housing for him and his family when he arrived in the United States and could he possibly help him out with the requirements.

A few weeks later, his friend wrote back stating that he found a farmer in the outskirts of Trenton who would be willing to provide a contract, but for a fee. I do not remember how much the fee was, only that my stepfather mailed him a check for the fee requested.

Several weeks later we received the farmer's contract agreement fulfilling the requirement.

My stepfather immediately took the contract to the American Consulate and after several weeks we were notified that we were approved to immigrate to the United States.

Once again, we had a lot to take care of and prepare for a long trip, especially since we needed to make our own travel arrangement.

After all was taken care of, we headed to the Fremantle Harbor, the port where we landed five years earlier. There we boarded a ship called the *Oronsay* a Cunard Line cruise ship and cruised toward the United States.

We departed from the Fremantle Harbor on November 5, 1955, and we cruised toward Sydney, Australia, where we stayed for one day to board more passengers.

The next day we departed from Sydney and cruised to Auckland, New Zealand and spent a day there, then it was on to Oceanic, Fiji Island, and after Fiji it was on to Honolulu, Hawaii.

While docked in Honolulu, I went strolling downtown with a Canadian girl I met on the ship along with an officer of the ship who offered to show us around the area, and while walking along the shopping area, all of a sudden the officer grabbed my arm and basically shoved me toward a store entrance where I fell to the floor.

The officer immediately followed me and helped me up while apologizing, then he proceeded to tell me that he was informed to be careful because there was an alert on the ship that young women were being kidnapped around the Honolulu area and because he heard a screeching car coming from behind us and because I was walking on the outer side of the street, he did not want me to become a statistic.

After that episode I was quite shaken up and decided to return to the ship and stay there the rest of the day.

The next morning we arrived in Vancouver, Canada. Vancouver is a lovely city with a lot of history. While there I was able to take a tour bus around town.

The following morning we arrived in San Francisco, California, our destination to disembark.
This was on December 8, 1955. After we collected all of our luggage, we made arrangements to transfer

everything to the train station for the cross-country train ride to Trenton, New Jersey.

All in all, the cruise was a wonderful experience for me, but most of all a much overdue vacation for my parents.

Australia truly is a lovely country with wonderful people, and I will always remember Australia with very fond memories.

47

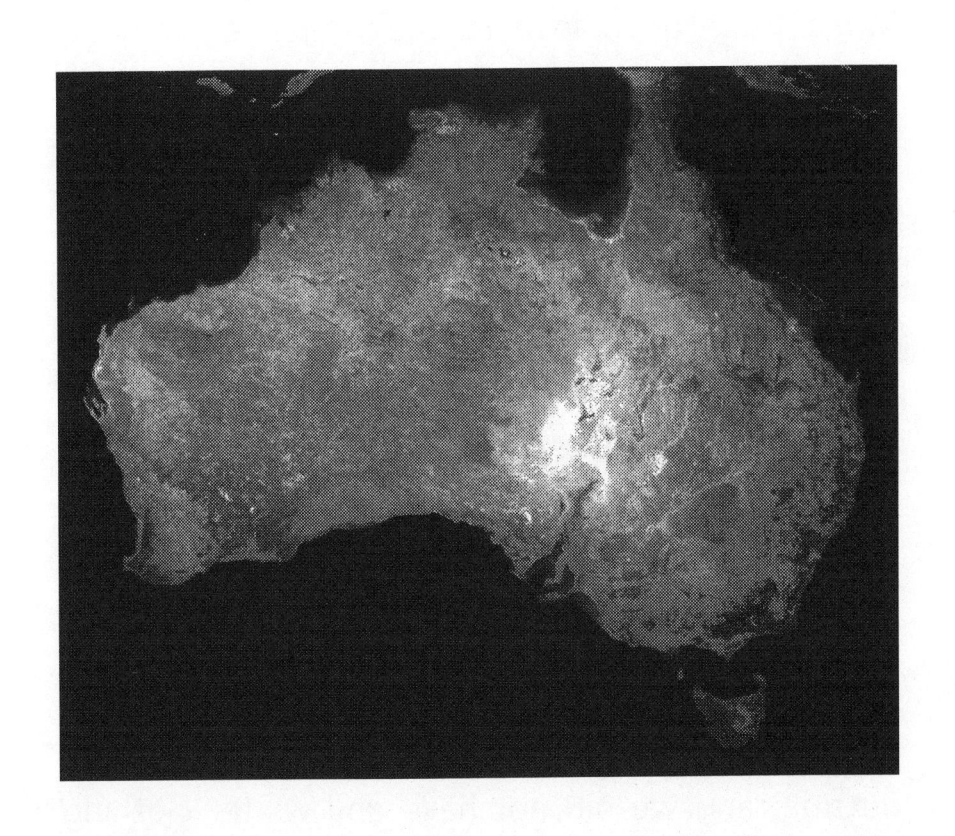

IMMIGRATING TO THE USA

As we arrived at the train station in Trenton, New Jersey, my stepfather's friend was there to welcome us.

The first thing he told my stepfather was that the farmer would not hold him to the contract agreement, unless he and the family wanted to stay at the farm, and that he was free to do whatever he wanted.
This really pleased my stepfather a lot. His friend further stated that there was a wrought iron company in West Trenton where he could apply for a job and that he also prenegotiated the rental of a two-bedroom semidetached home not far from him.

After settling in for a few days and getting oriented, my stepfather went to the wrought iron company to apply for work and was hired that week.

Only now we had one problem, it was cold and snowing outside, and we did not have any winter clothing to wear due to that fact that Australia was a warm-climate country.

Therefore, my mother and I took the bus into town to shop for winter items.

As we got off the bus I told my mother that since I spent all of my cash, I was going to go to a bank and open a savings account with my check from my previous account in Australia, shop, and I would see her later on at home.

I walked into the first bank I came to and requested to open a savings account with my check, plus withdraw one hundred dollars.
However, the new accounts clerk informed me that he was unable to do that because my check was in pounds and shillings, which is considered foreign currency. Therefore, they would have to send my check to the New York Foreign Exchange Commission and that could take up to ten days.

Naturally, this was very upsetting for me. I began to explain to him that I only needed one hundred dollars from my total amount because I needed to buy some winter clothing since I had just arrived two weeks ago from Australia, which is a warmer climate.

He then referred me to a senior officer of the bank.

The senior bank officer basically told me the same story, and once again I proceeded to inform him why

I desperately only needed one hundred dollars from my money.

After some consideration he stated that he would allow me the hundred dollars, but that the rest would not be available to me until collected and converted to U.S. currency.

Then he requested that I show him some identification plus he also had me sign a new account signature card and a hundred dollar withdrawal slip.

While processing all the paperwork, the senior officer began questioning me about my background and he asked me if I had ever considered working in a bank, to which I replied that I had not because in Australia you have to be a naturalized citizen to work in a bank, which I was not.

The officer then informed me that in the United States one was not required to be a naturalized citizen.

He then stood up and requested that I follow him because he would like for me to meet someone.

The person he wanted me to meet turned out to be the bank president. After more questioning he offered me a job at the bank and requested that I report to his office at eight o'clock in the morning in two days, which I accepted.

I then received the hundred dollars, thanked both officers and the clerk and went shopping.

Since I needed to look for a job anyway, this would help me for the time being. If I did not like the job, I could look for another while still working.

During those interviews, I never gave it a thought that the officer was actually lending me the hundred dollars. I was just too determined to get some cash somehow.

Two days later when I reported to the president's office, he informed me that he would take me to a branch office where I will receive instructions and training for the job.

We arrived at the branch office which was a large two-story building. The first floor was a regular bank branch office and the second floor was the operation processing center. The president took me up to the second floor and told me to take a seat. As I looked around I noticed that the operators were all punching various codes.

When the president returned, he introduced me to the manager and instructed him to train me.

I turned to the president and said, "Sir, I have only been in this country three weeks, I am still getting to know the area, and I am certainly not qualified to do this type of work." With this he turned to me and sternly said, "You can learn, can't you?" He then turned around and walked away and left me there.

Well, I did learn.

I guess his tone intimidated me.

However, after a while, I was not happy sitting behind one of those big machines punching numbers and codes all day.

Therefore, I called the president's office to make an appointment.

When I arrived at his office, I explained to him that I sincerely appreciated his help but that I was not happy punching buttons all day long; therefore, I wanted to give him a month's notice. He then asked me what I was looking for, to which I replied that I needed more variety type of work.

"Well," he said, "you need variety. Come with me I will get you variety."

He then drove me to another branch office, introduced me to the office manager, and instructed him to train me to become a teller and once again he turned around and left me there.

The bank president certainly was a well-meaning person but also a very blunt and stern person in his ways.

As before, I learned and became a teller. I must admit that the position did offer variety as well as contact with many nice people.

I also would like to point out that the bank was a local community bank where all the employees were from local areas, and the bank's board of directors were all from local surrounding area corporations, not like so many large conglomerate banks these days.

After some time later, I was promoted to head teller, then to branch manager, and assistant cashier. Eventually, I was promoted to assistant vice president and subsequently to vice president and manager of the main office.

During those years with the bank, I continuously enrolled in numerous specialized bank courses, and I also became involved with many various organizations. In some of the organizations I was just a member, but in some of the organizations I went through the chairs ending up as the president. A list of the organizational affiliations is listed in the end of this book.

Over the years, my experience at the bank was mostly very enjoyable. However, I did have some tense moments of which two were somewhat threatening and scary.

For instance at a small branch office, on a Saturday morning while sitting at my desk I observed three men walking toward the front entrance glass door, holding shotguns. I immediately hit the silent alarm button, and no sooner had I done that, when one of the men walked up to me, grabbed me by the collar of my blazer, and dragged me out to the center of the floor lobby and told me to stay there and not move.

At the same time one held the tellers at gunpoint and the third jumped over the counter and cleaned out the teller drawers.

On another occasion a few years later, while I was working at the operation processing center office, three men entered the office on the first floor while I was sitting in my office with a customer and yelled, "Nobody move."

One walked into my office and held me and the customer at gunpoint; another held all the tellers at gunpoint while the third jumped over the counter and robbed all the tellers.

Fortunately, in the holdups I was involved with, no one was ever hurt. I always periodically at staff meetings trained my staff that if involved in a holdup to never make any kind of move or motion or try to be a hero, unless you are ordered to, then do whatever they ask you to do. That way no one gets hurt or starts a shoot out.

Certainly, credit also goes to the police department who always were very professional.

They never entered the office during a holdup, unless they would hear gunfire. Instead they would camouflage around the building and wait until the robbers left. Then they would go after them and arrest them.

In the cases I was involved in, the robbers were always caught and prosecuted.

During my years in banking, I also had some fun times on weekends, going to movies with friends or a show in New York City or even a local dance.

Local dances were very popular during the fifties and that is how and where I met my husband. I must admit, he was the best that ever happened to me. He was not only kind and smart but also in support of all my endeavors, although he himself had a very busy schedule.

During the week he was a teacher of Special Education and on weekends he performed as a musician with a local band.

As a matter of fact, he previously performed with several known entertainers in some western states which involved a lot of traveling, but after a period of time he decided to take a break and go back home to his family.

After we were married, we first lived in a second floor apartment for a couple of years.
Then we purchased a small ranch home on a small lot.

Several years later as we were driving home from a friend's house, we noticed a house for sale on the way which we fell in love with.

Therefore, I made an appointment with the bank president to inquire if there was any possible chance for us to get some type of bridge loan using our present home as collateral which had improved quite a bit until sold.

The bank president informed me that he would send an appraiser to the house to evaluate the property then get back to me.

Several days later, the bank president called me and stated that the property was well worth looking into and that the bank would approve a bridge loan along with our present home until it is sold.

If it were not for the considerate bank president, I do not believe we would have been able to accomplish this.

Fortunately, everything worked out very well for us. Our ranch was sold in three months and we were able to renegotiate the financing.

Our new house was built on five acres with a natural creek running across the front of the property and then across the street through a golf course. The name of the creek was "Rancokas Creek."

All of the rooms were large plus it had a two-car garage and a two-car carport downstairs, along with an apartment with a separate entrance by the carport.

Because the house was built into a hillside, you walked up a flight of stairs in the front and ground level in the back and above the carport was a huge balcony enclosed with nine sets of sliding doors. (see picture)

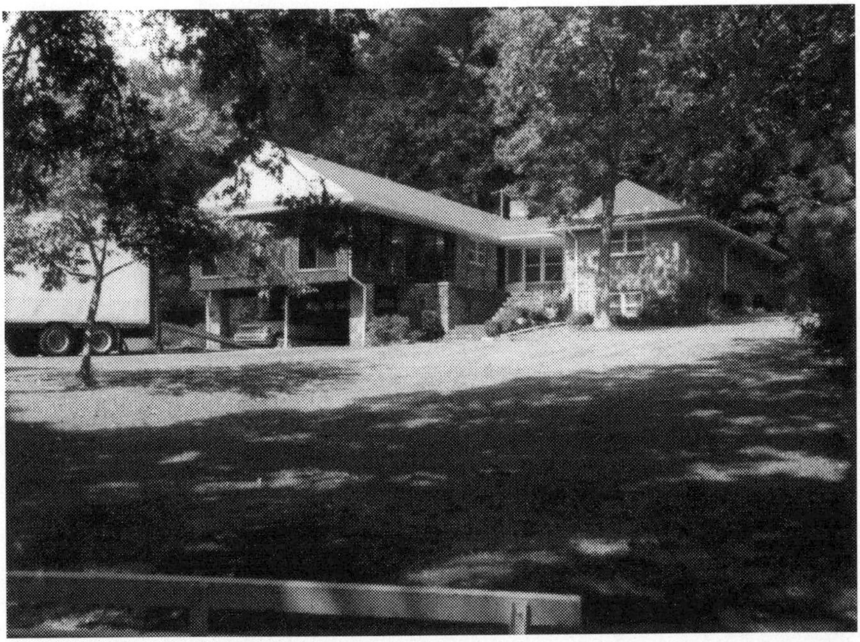

Shortly after having moved into our new home did we learn that all the stone and marble the house was built from was from a church fire in Trenton, New Jersey where two people perished.

Some builder hauled all of the salvaged material from the church to the area and built six homes all around the area.

Many times when we would try to plant a tree or a bush, the shovel would hit a stone or marble buried in the ground.

The property certainly was a lot of work and maintenance, but it also served us as a place of solitude where we recharged with a feeling of a getaway for many years.

Eventually banking entered a time when many were selling, merging, or being taken over by large corporate banks, and many senior officers opted to retire.

The bank I worked for was taken over by the First Jersey National Bank or North Jersey. Then only about two years later, they sold us to a British bank called The National Westminster Bank, and about five years later they decided to close in New Jersey and sold us to the Bank of America.

However, before all of the sale was totally finalized I retired. My husband at that time had already been retired for a couple of years, and we have had previous discussions about us moving to a warmer climate and a smaller home as we get older with less maintenance. This was now possible.

As we began to prepare to sell our house, which took a lot of work and time because we had to eliminate a lot of items which we would no longer need.

After all that was accomplished, we hired a real estate agent, and while the house was up for sale, we traveled to Orlando, Florida to shop for a home.

We selected Orlando because we had vacationed there several times and liked the area.

After our home in New Jersey was sold, we moved to Orlando, Florida to enjoy our retirement.

A few years later, we received a phone call from my mother-in-law, who was in her nineties and still living by herself in a small house. She informed us that she could no longer take care of everything and needed help, could she possibly come and live with us? Naturally, we told Mom that she would be welcome to come and stay with us.

She also informed us that her daughter's house was not large enough for her to move in with them and that she did not want to move into a senior housing complex.

At that time my husband informed his mother knowing how fond she always was of her daughter, that

first: she needs to discuss her decision with her
second: because of her age we will not fly her back and forth to visit
third: that she should seriously think about this for a few days to make sure she can live with those rules, then get back to us.

Mom called us back after a few days and told us that she did what we requested of her and she still wants to come down here to be with us.

My husband informed his mother that we needed a few days to empty one of our rooms so that we could ship her bedroom set down for her comfort, and we needed to board our pet dog, plus it would take us a couple of days to drive up there.

Because Mom had mentioned that she could not do a lot of walking, we purchased a wheelchair to take with us.

When we arrived at her house it was not in the best condition. Fortunately, her house was only a small five-room home with a separate one-car garage. After we prepared the house to sell, we engaged a real estate agent.

The realtor informed my husband that he will have to first make arrangements to get a home inspection certificate which is a state regulation. Also since he was hiring her, she advised him to get a power of attorney in order to avoid any hassles or technical problems.

After the home inspection was completed, we were told that the house and the garage had termite infestation, plus the electric wiring in the basement laundry area and the electric wiring to the garage from the house was in violation and would have to be redone.

While all of the violations were being taken care of, Mom's grandson approached my husband and told him that he wanted to purchase Mom's house.

My husband had no objection to his proposal, but since it was his mother's house and not his, he told Mom about the proposal. However, his mother told him that she did not want to sell the house to anyone in the family in order not to create problems.

However, when he told the grandson of Mom's decision, he and his mother became very upset about this and it created a lot of anger and anti-Semitism between us. But as I stated before, it was Mom's house and my husband would not overrule her decision.

While all this was happening, I received a phone call from my sister with some bad news. My sister was informing me that my mother received a call from the doctor's office this morning informing her that her cancer tests came back positive and that she would only have about one year to live.

Since it was fall with winter just around the corner, I suggested to my mother that she should come down to Florida for the winter and stay with us because we have three bedrooms where everyone would have their own room. Luckily she accepted my offer.

The next day I proceeded to get my mother checked by a cancer specialist to get another diagnosis, but unfortunately we received the same bad news.

Since my sister was still working at the time and living with my mother, she would take care of the home over the winter.

During the next two weeks while I was at my mother's home, my husband was taking care of matters at his mother's home.
He called his sister and requested that she come to Mom's house and take the cedar chest which Mom packed for her with some of the family heirlooms, plus take anything else she would like because we were only going to take Mom's bedroom set. Anything left would then be donated to the Salvation Army.

After all the violations were addressed, we contacted the realtor.

It did not take excessively long for the house to be sold. After which we prepared to leave for Florida, but the day before we left I went to see my mother and told her to allow me a little time to get Mom settled in, then I would come up to get her.

My mother told me that there was no need for me to come and get her and that she would fly down in two weeks.

The day we returned to Orlando, late that afternoon, the moving company delivered Mom's bedroom set which gave us time to set up her room and get her settled in.

Two weeks later my mother arrived and we got her settled in.

Thank the Lord, even though they always got along all right in the past, they were getting along just fine in the close quarters. Besides that they became company for each other.

We also visited Disney and Seaworld a couple of times and we spent some time at our Home Community Center, which they enjoyed relaxing by the pool.

Sadly, only a little over four months, my mother became very ill and was also in a lot of pain to the point where she could not get out of bed or walk. Therefore, we had her admitted to the hospital which recommended that we have her admitted to a nursing home. After we admitted her into a nursing home, she passed away only a few weeks later. This in a way was a blessing because of all the pain and medication she endured.

After we took care of my mother's funeral arrangements, we gradually adjusted our lives and for a while everything went along quite well. Only now Mom was spending all of her time with us which was basically all right, but I felt that she also needed some type of outside social connection with people her own age.

Therefore, I did some research to see if I could find some senior gathering group, and by luck I found one which I felt was nice. It was held at a church not far from us and it was called the Senior Social Group that met three times a week from 11:00 a.m. until 2:00 p.m. on Mondays, Wednesdays, and Fridays.
Mondays 11:00 a.m. to 12:00 p.m. was craft day, lunch 12:00 p.m. to 1:00 p.m. and 1:00 p.m. to 2:00 p.m. was social and relaxation time.

Wednesday 11:00 a.m. to 12:00 p.m. was entertainment day with someone playing the piano or a guest speaker, lunch 12:00 p.m. to 1:00 p.m., and 1:00 p.m. to 2:00 p.m. social and relaxation time.

Fridays 11:00 a.m. to 12:00 p.m. was a socializing time, lunch 12:00 p.m. to 1:00 p.m., and 1:00 p.m. to 2:00 p.m. was special dessert time and relaxation.

I registered Mom for the Wednesday session only to see if she would enjoy attending. When I told Mom that I registered her at a Church Senior Social Club, she did not want to go, but I insisted that I wanted her to just attend one meeting, and if she did not like it or enjoy herself, she did not have to go back again.

When I went to pick up Mom after her first meeting attendance, to my surprise she was all excited and began to tell me that she would also like to attend the Friday meeting because one of the ladies told her that they served delicious desserts. She further asked me to go shopping with her to buy a few new items to wear.

Of course I was happy to oblige and to see her enjoying herself.

This also gave us a little more time to get some things done.

This schedule worked out quite well for some time.

At that time I also hired a once-a-week visiting nurse to check Mom's vital signs, give her a bath or shower and shampoo, plus cut both her fingernails and toenails when needed.

One night while Mom was getting ready to go to sleep, I noticed that she had tears in her eyes. I asked her what was troubling her and she said to me that it saddens her that her daughter never sent her a birthday or Mother's Day card nor even calls her to see how she is doing. I told Mom that she should call her and ask her, but Mom's reply was "I am the mother and she should call me."

There was no point in us calling because they would not talk to us anyway.

When Mom reached the age of ninety-eight she started to slow up quite a lot and she began to be forgetful.

Sometimes, she would wake us up in the middle of the night and ask us where she had to go?

The visiting nurse recommended that we take Mom to the doctor's office and have her checked out. She also recommended that if the analysis is to admit Mom into a nursing home, we should make certain it accepts Medicaid because if they do not, then they will just transfer Mom to one that did when her finances run out.

After we took Mom to the doctor, he advised us that we should admit Mom into a nursing home for her own safety.

While checking several nursing homes, we found that the one my mother was in some time ago was not as fancy as some others, but it was always clean and neat and it accepted Medicaid. In case her finances were depleted, she would then not be transferred to some other available place. Therefore, we made arrangements to have her admitted.

We also set up a visitation schedule to make certain that Mom would be cared for properly. We both visited her daily, but not together, instead alternately and also at different times. This way the nursing home never knew when one of us would show up.

Many people are aware that nursing homes are not cheap. Mom was not a wealthy person, therefore, we wanted to make sure if admitted she would not be moved to another facility when her finances run out and changed to Medicaid coverage.

She lived in the nursing home for a period of time and passed away peacefully at the age of ninety-nine and a half.

Since Mom had a prepaid cemetery plot with her husband in New Jersey, we needed to have her body prepared and flown to New Jersey where we held a viewing, a church service, and a burial service at the cemetery.

Many relatives and friends attended the services, but sadly her daughter did not attend any. After all the funeral services were taken care of, we returned to Florida, and one month later the funeral director mailed us a picture to show and prove to us that Mom's name and dates were engraved on the tombstone.

Then less than a year later my sister called me to tell me that she was going to retire and that she was going to sell the house in New Jersey and move down here to be near us.

After she retired I flew to New Jersey to assist her to accomplish everything and drove my mother's car down to Florida, where she is living in her own house a couple of blocks away and enjoying her retirement.

Somehow, something always seems to happen from time to time, no matter what.

Only two years later my sister was diagnosed with breast cancer stage three and would require chemo and radiation treatments, plus surgery after that.

After the completion of all the above, she was doing quite well, with some minor limitations and only has to get checked twice a year by the cancer doctor.
As a matter of fact she just received a clean bill of health a few months ago, and I am truly grateful because she is the only close relative I have.

Then a few years later my husband was diagnosed with kidney failure, and shortly thereafter needed to go for daily dialysis treatments. After only six months of dialysis he passed away, one month after we celebrated our fifty-fifth anniversary.

This was a very difficult and sad time in my life, and I still miss him terribly. He truly was my soul mate, but now God has him in his keeping and I have him in my heart.

As I reflect back over my life, I must have had a guardian angel watching over me.
I survived the turbulence of World War II, uprooted to two lovely countries, launched an accidental banking career, and married a wonderful partner.

Fortunately, I still have my sister, many wonderful friends, and some organizational involvements, all of which help to keep me active.

It is just a shame that after the war, I only had two uncles left. One was my father's brother who passed away a long time ago, although he had a son with whom I lost contact over the years. The other was my mother's brother, who was a typical Nazi officer, who threatened to sever his relationship with us if my mother married my potential stepfather.

Since my mother went ahead and married my stepfather anyway, he totally severed his association with us thereafter.

As far as my husband's family is concerned, somehow when his mother decided to come and live with us, the animosity still exists, and I am not in contact with them although, I do hear from some of his distant relatives.

In ending, I wish to mention that to this day I never watch any type of war movies or programs; they open too many bad memories.

"I ALWAYS TRY TO REMEMBER"

THAT SOMETIMES LIFE THROWS US UNEXPECTED CURVES.

SOME ARE GOOD
AND
SOME ARE NOT

IT IS ALL IN WHAT WE MAKE OF IT, AND WE MUST DEAL WITH THEM WITH DETERMINATION TO DO THE BEST WE CAN, NO MATTER WHAT.

* * * * * *

My mother, sister, and I

IN MEMORY OF FRANK ISITORO

December 27, 1929–November 22, 2013

He was born in Brooklyn, New York, and raised in Trenton, New Jersey. In later years he lived in Jacobstown, New Jersey, until moving to Orlando, Florida.

He served in the U.S. Army 9th INF Division where he was assigned to the Division Military Band Unit serving as first chair in the marching and concert bands. When his service time expired, he received an honorable discharge and an offer to join the West Point Military Band, but he decided to turn that down because his desire was to travel the USA a bit and perform professionally. He had the pleasure of working with Ralph Flanagan's Orchestra, the Chuck Cabot Orchestra, Nelson Eddie, Patty Page, and Maguire Sisters Shows, plus many others. A graduate from the College of New Jersey, he began a career in Elementary Education, later switching to Special Education, and retired from the Pembertown Township School District of New Jersey.

Frank was an avid golfer and a professional trombone and vibraphone player forming his own group called, "Music by Frank Benedict and his Orchestra," he performed at the New Hope Playhouse Inn, New Hope, New Jersey; the Princeton Inn's Yankee Doodle University Room, Princeton, New Jersey; and at the Atlantic City Steel Peer.

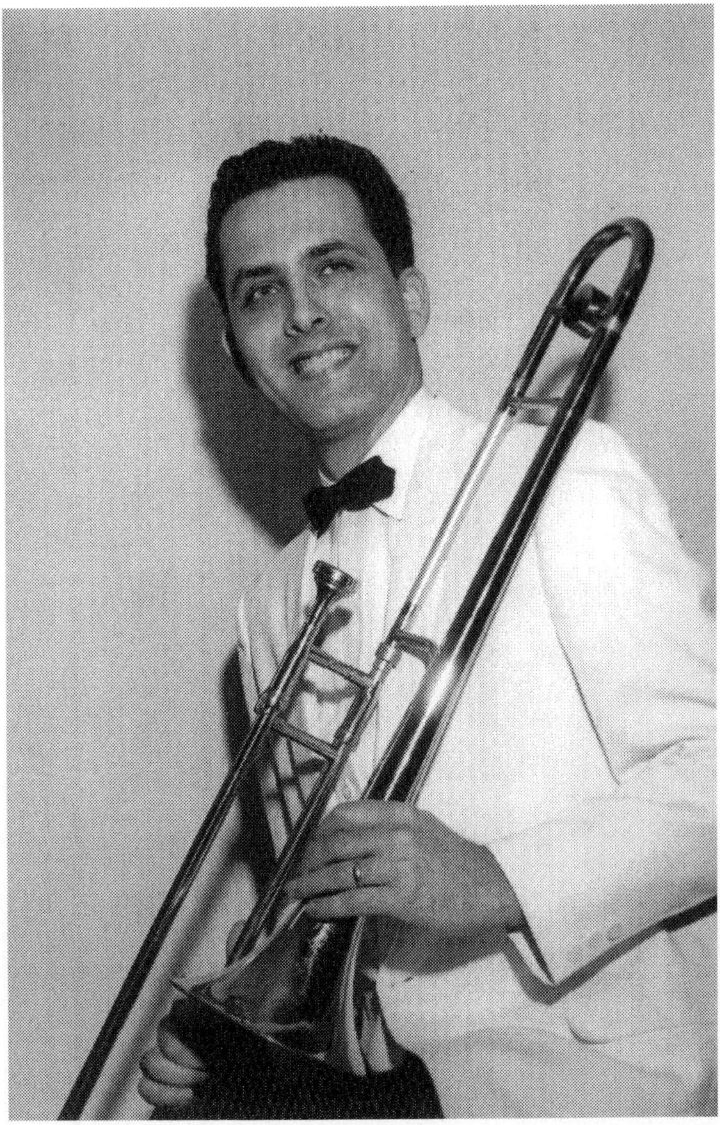

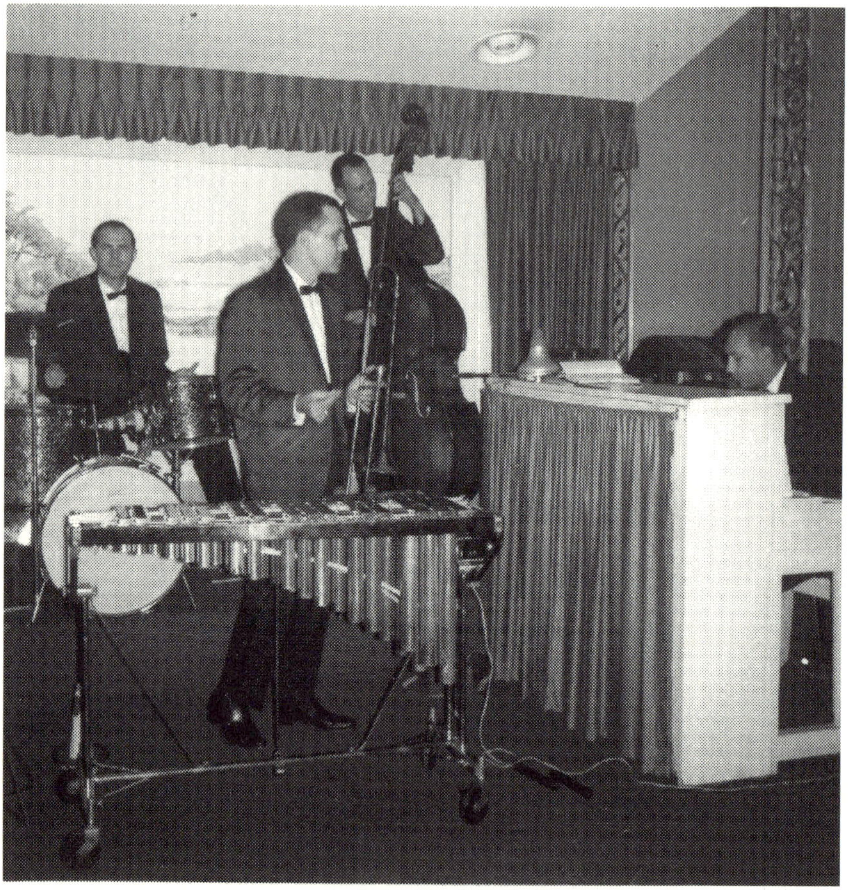

Isabella Isitoro

ASK A BUSY PERSON

Isabella Isitoro

In December 1955 Isabella Isitoro, newly arrived in Trenton from Perth, Australia, set out to open an account at a local bank, stopping at the first one she passed, The Broad Street National.

Little did she know that 25 years later she would be an assistant vice president of the same bank.

"After filling out the forms and some discussion, I was asked if I were looking for a job. I completed an application and was hired. At that time I really had no intention of making a career of it," she says.

In December 1955 Isabella Isitoro, newly arrived in Trenton from Perth, Australia, set out to open an account at a local bank, stopping at the first one she passed, The Broad Street National.

Little did she know that twenty-five years later she would be an assistant vice president of the same bank.

"After filling out the forms and some discussion, I was asked if I were looking for a job. I completed an application and was hired. At that time I really had no intention of making a career of it," she says.

A career, however, it has become, and today Isabella Isitoro is the manager of the bank's Whitehead Road office.

Although she can't recall feeling discriminated against during her years in banking, Isitoro says, "There was a time when it seemed to be an accepted fact that women never rose above the position of teller. Banking has really opened up for women in the last five years."

The reason for much of this, she believes, is the merit of women today who are "much more career-minded and inclined toward a dual lifestyle, rather than one of simply being a housewife."

Citing today's economic situation, she says that to maintain a certain standard of living, women realize that they must work and "figure they might as well make it a career."

As far as management is concerned, Isitoro feels that today in banking most people don't think in terms of men's or women's positions but rather consider what a person is capable of doing.

Her own career in banking has been one of steady advancement. Although originally hired for the bank's transit department which deals mainly with paperwork, she quickly moved to a teller position because she preferred meeting the public.

Selected by the bank for its management training program, she was promoted from head teller to assistant branch manager in its western office. In September 1979 she became the Whitehead Road office's branch manager, and in June 1979 was named an assistant vice president.

Her position with the bank has led to her involvement with the Mercer County Chamber of Commerce, and this year she is chairman of the Lawrence Action Council. The monthly meetings she sees as an important opportunity for businesses to exchange information.

Describing the action council as the community's link to the chamber, she uses as an example its education committee which is working with the Lawrence Township School System and Notre Dame High School on a cooperative education program which attempts to place students in part-time positions with local businesses.

"This is really a worthwhile program," she says. "Many of the part-time jobs become full-time ones after graduation. It also gives the students important experience."

Isitoro is also the vice chairman and program director for the Capitol Group of the National Association of Bank Women Officers. She is a past president of the Trenton Chapter of the American Institute of Banking (AIB), an affiliate of the New Jersey Bankers Association.

The AIB offers a program of banking courses taught by local bankers specializing in particular areas. The program is very extensive. In 1975, when she was its vice president and education director, the enrollment was four hundred.

She speaks positively about her field, although she has experienced five holdups. She says that after each one she contemplated giving up banking, "but the love of working with and helping people keeps me here."

The demands of her job leave her little free time. "My husband Frank is very understanding," she says with a smile. When the weather permits, she enjoys gardening at their home. She also works in ceramics when she has the time. "For me it's a release, a time to concentrate on just one thing and relax," she says.

Anne M. Dorlon

I was one of 37 local business leaders to be invited by The State of New JerseyDepartment of Defense to visit the Peterson Air Force Base Academy and NORAD on Aug.22-23,1984 in Colorado Springs, Colorado

I was one of 12 local business leaders to be invited by The State of New Jersey, Department of Defense to visit the U.S. Air Force Air National Guard Military Education Center on 9/27/10984 in Tennessee

Trenton Police Athletic Award
January 21, 1993

City of Trenton Special Award
January 30, 1993

1960	New Jersey Bankers Association Member
1972 *	Broad St. National Bank Employee Award
1974	New Jersey Notary Association Member and Notary Public Appointment
1975 *	Broad St. National Bank Employee Award
1976	New Jersey Institute of Banking Member
1977	New Jersey Institute of Banking President (recruited senior bankers from various banks to narrate business meeting)
1978	American Institute of Banking Member
1979	American Institute of Banking President (set up various bank-related courses for bank employees and recruit senior bank officers as the instructors)
1980	Mercer County Chamber of Commerce

Member
(+ was interviewed for an article in the Mercer Business monthly magazine, copy enclosed in this narrative)

1980 The Lawrence Township Council
Member
(assisted with the Lawrence School System Exchange program to place students into clerical positions)

1980 National Association of Bank Women Officers
Member

1981 National Association of Bank Women Officers
President
(recruited senior officers to teach various bank officers advanced bank-related subjects)

1982 Mercer County Chamber of Commerce
President
(planned monthly business speaker related luncheons for business CEOs)

1983	Mercer County Business Association Member
1984	State of New Jersey - County of Mercer received an invitation to visit NORAD and the Peterson Air Force base located in Colorado. (as a guest along with other local business owners)
1985	State of New Jersey, County of Mercer received an invitation to visit the U.S. National Air Force Guard Academy and the Air National Guard Military Education Center located in Tennessee. (as a guest along with other local business owners)
1986	DVUW (Delaware Valley United Way) (I was loaned to them by the bank to assist with the annual campaign activities.)
1986	New Jersey Women's Network, Princeton, New Jersey Member
1987*	The First Jersey National Bank

Employee Award

1988   New Jersey Association of Bank Women Officers
President
(planned monthly business speaker luncheons for various bank women officers)

1989*   The National Westminster Bank Employee Award

1990   The Trenton Y.W.C.A.
Member

1990   The Trenton Police Athletic League
Chairperson
(planned monthly business speaker luncheons for the league members and assist with children athletic ctivities)

1991   American Cancer Society
(I was a loaned bank executive for the Annual Cancer Campaign)

1992   The Trenton Consumer Business Bureau

(I was a loaned bank executive to set up business narrated meetings for business owners)

1993 The Contemporary Club in Trenton Member

1993 The City of Trenton appointed me chairman of the city's Annual Easter Parade